8/30/2018

Dear Jim and Jann,

It's incredible that you are celebrating 60 years of togetherness! What a wonderful example for all of us. Congratulations,

We are all So grateful for you Both!

Bonnie also wanted "do 60 years"

Love you, Kelli

MW00713245

-8-30-18

Alles Gute!
Lothar

Tammy
-N-
Jim
Randle
@ 42 years!

Elaina

GOOD ✦ OLD ✦ DAYS

Live It Again™
1958

Dear Friends,

Dick Clark, host of television's *American Bandstand* show, knew early on that rock 'n' roll had an irresistible appeal for America's young. It was a style of music that urged listeners to respond by whirling, shaking, stomping and clapping their way through the latest hits. Yes, in 1958, we loved to dance. The hand jive was a dance phenomenon in the summer of 1958 and chances are if you danced, you still remember the moves. The dance, consisting of various hand movements done in a pattern, was easy to learn and a whole lot of fun. Even young married couples with preschool children managed to carve out an evening now and then to swing to the music.

Young and old alike, we were enthralled by the Westerns that dominated the top spots on television, viewed in over 42 million homes. We religiously followed the plots of *Gunsmoke*, *Wagon Train* and *Maverick*, cheering on the good guys and rejoicing in the demise of the criminals. The western influence was reflected in children's toys, as well. Toy chests included dress-up costumes inspired by heroes Zorro, Hopalong Cassidy or Annie Oakley that stimulated children's imagination and fun.

The hand jive was a dance phenomenon in the summer of 1958.

With the launch of Explorer 1, America's first satellite, on January 31st, we were rocketed into the Space Age. President Eisenhower established the National Aeronautics and Space Administration and the race to explore space and all its mysteries was on. We were consumed with curiosity about what lay beyond the fringes of Earth's atmosphere.

Settle into your easy chair, put up those feet that danced with the best of them, and relive 1958 through this edition of *Live It Again*. It was a year that included heartthrob Elvis Presley's induction into the Army, breathlessly followed by legions of teenage girls, and the birth of the Hula-Hoop™, a top-selling toy. Dream of your youthful exploits, or read this book to tune in to what made the year an important part of the fabulous fifties for those who lived it. Enjoy!

Contents

© 1958

1958 Quiz

1. What was the original name of Alka-Seltzer's mascot, Speedy?

2. What racehorse won both the Kentucky Derby and Preakness Stakes?

3. Who was the first African American female to compete in national and international tennis?

4. What famous singing star joined the Army in March 1958?

5. What automobile was known as the most notorious pratfall?

6. What was President Eisenhower's dog's name?

7. Who was the winning quarterback in the NFL championship game?

8. What singing duo made "All I Have to Do Is Dream" famous?

Answers appear on page 127

Dick Clark's *American Bandstand* ran on afternoon network television. The show provided a way for teens—and probably a healthy number of adults—all over the country to learn the latest dance steps.

High school prom was the most anticipated social event of the year. The gym was transformed into a wonderland filled with boys in suits and ties, and girls in colorful dresses with full skirts.

That first junior high dance was generally not an event of grace and elegance, especially when the girl was a head taller.

We Loved to Dance

Care to dance? Just like in previous years, most Americans enjoyed any event that involved dancing. The bop, stroll and hand jive were trendy styles of dance. Rock the night away to a live band, or make sure you're somewhere with one of those vital devices—a juke box or record player. Shaking their hips and singing along, young people from junior high through college celebrated their freedom from strait-laced traditions. When the band played a more romantic number, slow dancing ruled, sometimes to the consternation of attending chaperones and other adults. When rock 'n' roll was played, it electrified the feet and rattled the brain. There was a whole lot of shaking going on.

Elderly matrons taught the young men the basics of the box step.

©GETTY IMAGES

©1958 SEPS

This couple practices the hand jive at home in preparation for Saturday night's dance when they hope to be the life of the party.

©2011 H. ARMSTRONG ROBERTS/CLASSICSTOCK

For a night out dancing, the only requirement was to be fit and willing, which was exactly how it should be.

The Top Music Makers

The rock 'n' roll era was in full swing. Contrary to popular belief, teenagers were not the sole audience, although they made up the majority. Persons of all age groups, from preschoolers to those with graying hair, were fans of rock 'n' roll. Entertainers were eliminating a lot of the yelling and screaming, and substituting good rhythms, beats and tunes that gave the genre a broader appeal. The sounds of the doo-wop quartet, Danny & the Juniors, filled the airwaves with the smash hit, "At the Hop." With its smooth, constant vocal harmonies, doo-wop was one of the most mainstreamed, pop-oriented rhythm and blues styles of 1958.

Tommy Edwards, singer and songwriter, was most remembered for his 1958 Billboard No. 1, "It's All in the Game." This song was an undisputable classic of its era, highlighted by Edwards' strong, masterful vocals.

Early in 1958, Dick Clark presented the group Danny & the Juniors with a gold record for the song "At the Hop" on *American Bandstand*, the first of many awards and accolades they would receive over the years.

Top Hits of 1958

"At the Hop"
Danny & the Juniors

"It's All in the Game"
Tommy Edwards

"The Purple People Eater"
Sheb Wooley

"All I Have to Do Is Dream"
The Everly Brothers

"Tequila"
The Champs

"Don't"
Elvis Presley

"Volare"
Domenico Modugno

"Sugartime"
The McGuire Sisters

"He's Got the Whole World in His Hands"
Laurie London

"The Chipmunk Song"
The Chipmunks

©GETTY IMAGES

The McGuire Sisters maintained a busy television schedule, making frequent appearances on popular variety shows. The trio was dressed and coiffed identically and performed their synchronized body movements and hand gestures with military precision.

©GETTY IMAGES

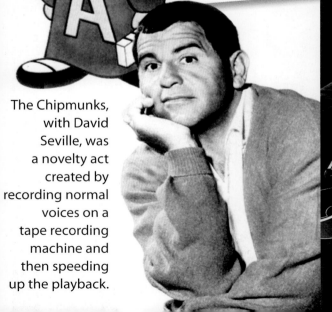

The Chipmunks, with David Seville, was a novelty act created by recording normal voices on a tape recording machine and then speeding up the playback.

The Everly Brothers were country-influenced rock 'n' roll performers, known for steel-string guitar playing and close harmony.

FAMOUS BIRTHDAYS

Lorenzo Lamas, January 20 actor (Lance of *Falcon Crest, California Fever*)

Judy Norton-Taylor, January 29 actress (Mary Ellen of *The Waltons*)

For $20, Ansco's Lancer camera kit included everything necessary for fine pictures—clip-on flash unit, four flash bulbs and one roll of Ansco film.

Bausch & Lomb advertised a slide projector that always stayed in focus and practically ran by itself with prices starting at $84.

Magic moments of memories would spring to life with brilliance, clarity and color when using the new movie projectors. This Keystone projector sold for $100.

For $29, photography buffs could buy this Anscoflex II camera with a close-up lens for portraits and built-in yellow filter to darken skies and brighten clouds. Also included were the case, flash unit, bulbs and two rolls of film.

The Newest in Home Entertainment

The quality of home movies improved in 1958. A peek at the meter and a twist of the lens was all that was required for perfectly exposed color movies in any kind of light. Some movie cameras featured wide-angle and telephoto lenses for unusual effects and sold for about $80. Everything necessary for fine photographs was available in both black and white or color. The Sears catalog provided fast photo development service for less than $1 a roll for black and white prints and from $1 to $2 for color prints and transparencies. Pocket-size transistor radios operated on flashlight batteries. Phonographs were portable with stylish, colorful cases.

Phonographs became portable with high-style fashion in dreamy colors. Sold for $23, this model was feminine with a quilt-padded exterior and gold handle.

1958 MONTGOMERY WARDS

1958 STROMBERG-CARLSON CORPORATION

COURTESY OF ZENITH

COURTESY OF ZENITH

New pocket-size transistor radios had vibrant tone and brought in many stations. The ultimate Zenith radio above was sold for $250 and was powered to tune in the world. It was able to receive standard broadcasts, international short wave, marine, weather and amateur receptions.

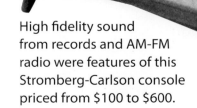

High fidelity sound from records and AM-FM radio were features of this Stromberg-Carlson console priced from $100 to $600.

This Philco television was so light and trim, it was like having a TV in a brief case. This model sold for about $180.

The Newest in Home Entertainment

Television sets

Sales of television sets continued to boom. In June of 1958, there were 42.4 million TV homes in the nation. With the flood of buyer's dollars, manufacturers competed to produce televisions with interesting, eye-catching features to lure buyers. Say goodbye to knobs and annoying out-of-focus TV. Tuning became automatic with one touch of a button. Living hi-fi pictures and complete sound systems were built in. One company even produced a television with the world's first separate screen. Owners could keep the set beside a chair and put the picture anywhere.

Admiral tempted buyers to upgrade to new models by offering trade-in allowances.

The RCA Victor TV remote was every man's dream come true, making it possible to relax anywhere in the room and still be in control.

Favorite shows could be viewed in living color. This RCA Victor Southbridge model retailed for $695.

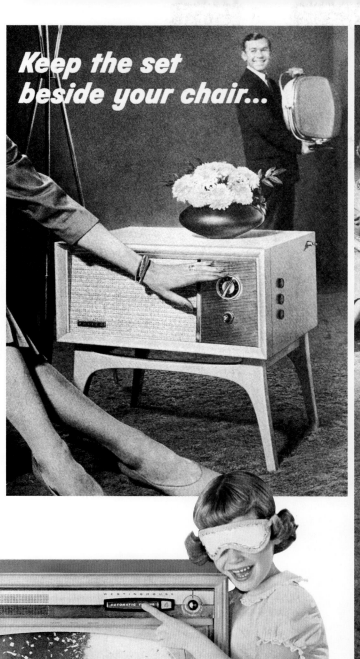

Keep the set beside your chair...

...put the picture anywhere!

Philco built the chassis and sound system of this model into an elegant end table for $339.95. It had a separate screen that could be moved around the room.

Westinghouse sold TVs that had automatic tuning, making changing channels easy even for children.

fresh fruit flavor
you can see!

tip the bottle...see the fruit

that gives you fresher flavor

The character "Little Squirt" was created in 1941 to use in marketing for the soft drink and the little tike encouraged people to "Drink Squirt."

To produce milk that meets first of all the health needs of tiny children

Elsie the cow debuted in 1939 as Borden's mascot for wholesome and healthy dairy products.

1958 Trivia

Q. When was Sunbeam White Bread first marketed?

A. In 1942, in the Philadelphia area, where it became an instant success.

The pretty blue-eyed blonde Sunbeam girl was Sunbeam Bread's recognizable mascot.

Brand-Name Mascots We Remember

Ah yes, we do love our mascots. Food mascots are some of the most recognizable images in advertising. Ever since the early days of eye-popping packaging and TV commercials, cartoon mascots have been used to promote memorable products. Antonio Gentile, an imaginative and artistic school boy, submitted a sketch to Planters' brand-icon contest in 1916. Gentile won the contest and Mr. Peanut became the nut company's official mascot. The recognizable Jolly Green Giant mascot was used even before the vegetable canning company was named Green Giant. Sunbeam bread's Miss Sunbeam was created in the early 1940s by Ellen Segner, a well-known children's book illustrator. The mascot was based on the artist's observation of a blond-haired, blue-eyed little girl playing in the park.

The Mr. Peanut mascot appeared on billboards, starred in television commercials and even earned a star on Madison Avenue's Advertising Walk of Fame.

With his impressive stature, green skin and toga-style outfit of leaves, it was hard to miss the Jolly Green Giant, known for presiding over vegetables grown in his valley since 1928.

…Relief is just a swallow away

SPEEDY

Alka-Seltzer

Speedy, the mascot for Alka-Seltzer, was created in 1951 and was originally named Sparky. The name was changed to coincide with the theme of Alka-Seltzer offering "speedy relief."

The Television Shows We Watched

1958 Debuts

The television detective show *Sea Hunt* debuted in January 1958. *TV Guide* called it "an epic so watery that Lloyd Bridges' colleagues tell him they have to drain their TV sets after watching his show." More than half of the show took place beneath the waves. *The Donna Reed Show*, a family comedy, was introduced and aired until 1966. The show had a wholesome quality that endeared it to audiences. *The Rifleman* was the saga of Lucas McCain, a homesteader in the Old West struggling to make a living off his ranch and make a man out of his motherless son. *Peter Gunn* was one of the first suave, lady-killer detective shows to be seen on television.

Lloyd Bridges starred in *Sea Hunt* as an ex-navy frogman who became a free-lance undersea investigator.

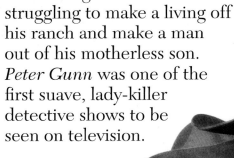

Chuck Connors starred as the widowed New Mexico rancher, Lucas McCain, and Johnny Crawford starred as his son, Mark, on *The Rifleman*.

THE WEATHER
City and Suburban—Rain,
Snow, Colder
Month in Delay Almanac

The Metro Daily News

VOLUME 41—No. 351

FINAL EDITION

20 PAGES

FIVE CENTS

JANUARY 29, 1958

ACTRESS JOANNE WOODWARD AND ACTOR PAUL NEWMAN WED

The wedding ceremony was held at Hotel El Rancho in Las Vegas, Nev.

The Donna Reed Show centered on model housewife and perfect mother, Donna Stone, her husband, Alex, a pediatrician, and their rambunctious kids, Mary and Jeff. Left to right: Shelley Fabares, Paul Peterson, Carl Betz and Donna Reed.

Peter Gunn star, Craig Stevens, worked to get his clients out of trouble and solve crimes, somehow always managing to come out on top.

Television Shows Debuting in 1958

Sea Hunt

Confession

Concentration

Peter Gunn

The Donna Reed Show

The Rifleman

The Huckleberry Hound Show

Encounter

Bat Masterson

77 Sunset Strip

An Evening With Fred Astaire

The Lawman

Tops on Television

Gunsmoke
CBS

Wagon Train
NBC

Have Gun Will Travel
CBS

The Rifleman
ABC

The Danny Thomas Show
CBS

Maverick
ABC

Tales of Wells Fargo
NBC

The Real McCoys
ABC

I've Got A Secret
CBS

The Life and Legend of Wyatt Earp
ABC

Gunsmoke stars are shown from left: Amanda Blake as Kitty Russell, James Arness as Marshal Matt Dillon, Dennis Weaver as Chester Goode and Milburn Stone as Dr. Galen 'Doc' Adams.

Walter Brennan starred in *The Real McCoys*, a show that became one of the biggest hits on TV.

The Television Shows We Watched

The top 10 in 1958

Westerns won the top spots in the 1958 show lineup. The shows featured rugged individuals and the plots were simple and to the point. Good always triumphed over evil and crime did not pay. The top show *Gunsmoke*, starring James Arness as Marshal Matt Dillon, started a deluge of westerns on television, but outlived them all. *Wagon Train* seemed to encompass the whole American West. It employed a big cast and was an hour long show in most seasons. *The Real McCoys* was a hit rural comedy that experts said would never work. Okay for the sticks, they wrongly surmised, but no good for city viewers. *Maverick*, broadcast on Sunday evenings, starring wise-cracking James Garner, was unique as a Western with a sense of humor.

Actors James Garner (top) and Jack Kelly playing in a scene for the TV show *Maverick*.

Actors Robert Horton, left, and Ward Bond, in a promotional portrait for the western television series, *Wagon Train*.

Ed Sullivan celebrates the 10th anniversary of his variety show, a Sunday night favorite.

Lawrence Welk, Mister Music Maker

Lawrence Welk's champagne music was first heard on national television in 1955. Welk went on to a 16-year network run on Saturday nights. The Welk formula was good, old-fashioned music straightforwardly presented. When Welk played his accordion or danced with one of the ladies in the audience, viewers loved it. Much of the appeal of the program lay with its close-knit family of performers. Probably the most famous of Welk's alumni were "da lovely Lennon Sisters," singers who stayed with the show for more than 12 years. Other favorites included accordionist Myron Floren, deep-voiced singer-pianist Larry Hooper, and dancers Bobby Burgess and Barbara Boylan. High point of the season was the annual Christmas show. Band members brought their families and their children were invited to perform for the program as well.

Welk interrupts a TV rehearsal to give autographs to Girl Scout visitors. Although his music was the direct opposite of rock 'n' roll, many teenagers liked him.

Bandleader Lawrence Welk with an assortment of items he gave away to fans during public appearances.

1958 Trivia

Q. When was Lawrence Welk born?

A. On March 11, 1903, in Strasburg, N.D.

At the Aragon Ballroom in Ocean Park, Calif., Welk dances with his "Champagne Lady," Alice Lon.

The four Lennon sisters flocking around Welk during a rehearsal lunch. They are Dianne (in pincurls, second from left), Janet, Peggy and Kathy.

FAMOUS BIRTHDAYS
Joe Frank Edwards Jr., February 3 astronaut
Kurt Rambis, February 25 NBA forward (Lakers, Hornets)

What Made Us Laugh

"My daddy always puts an olive in his tea."

"Boy, is he in a jam!"

"When do you go back to the beauty shop for a checkup?"

"Now, before I start, anyone who wishes to leave may do so. This is going to be no place for a coward."

"I still prefer to raid the icebox."

"You don't know my bridge club."

"I think the two weeks are beginning
to show on Airman Finley."

"Now when you're thoroughly at ease with the
cigarette lighter, we'll take up with the gears."

Ford's Edsel was touted for elegant styling and luxurious comfort, all for a moderate price starting at $3,500. But the car was over-advertised and did not meet buyer's expectations. It was the first victim of advertising hype.

Driving a Cadillac was to command the very finest i automotive performance. own a Cadillac was acquiri the most rewarding of personal possessions for a price ranging from $5,000 the way to a hefty $13,000 for a top-of-the-line mode

The new Chevrolet featured a gull-wing rear, body by Fisher, full coil suspension, solid road-gripping feel and advanced V8 engine for a moderate price.

Behind the Wheel

American advertising presented endless images of the good life. The excess of consumerism was present in all aspects of life, but was especially true of cars, the status symbol of the era. American manufacturers sent a loud and clear message to Americans: Cars are fun and they are fun to drive. Especially popular were big, long cars. Ford took one of the auto industry's most notorious pratfalls when it introduced the Edsel, an entirely new car division. It really wasn't a bad car. Ford's marketing people led the public to expect a wonder car, but buyers actually received much less. The sales reflected the disappointment.

© 1958 SEPS

A car salesman and buyer huddle under the hood to inspect the car's engine, while the woman is more concerned with the outward appearance.

REPRINTED WITH PERMISSION FROM GENERAL MOTORS COMPANY

Move up to an Oldsmobile, advertising beckoned, with its beautiful interiors and luxurious appointments, winning performance and prudent economy.

Advertisements suggested car buyers invest in the best with America's new fine-car style leader, the Chrysler Imperial. It was a comfort and luxury car that handled with ease and sold for about $5,000.

COURTESY OF CHRYSLER GROUP LLC

Behind the Wheel
Room for the family

1958 saw amazing growth in the station wagon. As families grew, so did their cars. Buy a Rambler, above, for about $2,500 and get the best of both American big-car comfort and European small-car economy. It set efficiency records with a cost of less than a penny a mile using regular gasoline. The term "gas-guzzler" was already being used in 1958.

The Pontiac station wagon was a bold new car for a bold new generation.

REPRINTED WITH PERMISSION FROM THE WISCONSIN HISTORICAL SOCIETY & CNH AMERICA, LLC

Equipped with extra safety and convenience features, International's Travelall could transport eight adults or a gang of little ones. It could haul a "wagon" load with space to spare.

The swept-wing Sierra by Dodge was called a "land yacht" and cost more than other body styles, starting at $2,700. This model had a one-piece tailgate with a rear-facing, rear-entry third seat that could be flipped forward to create more cargo room.

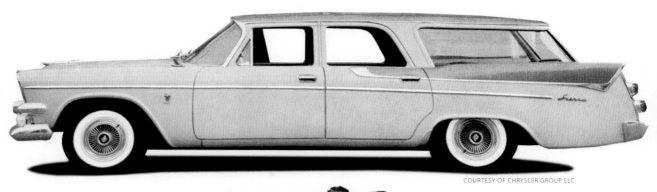

COURTESY OF CHRYSLER GROUP LLC

REPRINTED WITH PERMISSION FROM GENERAL MOTORS COMPANY

Chevrolet's station wagon was dramatically lower, wider and nine inches longer. The lift gate was hinged into the roof and raised completely out of the way for easier loading.

Oldsmobile station wagons were advertised as being the family-fun way to go places in the "Rocket Age." With slim, sleek lines and an elegant interior, this vehicle was also rugged and ready for any load or road.

REPRINTED WITH PERMISSION FROM GENERAL MOTORS COMPANY

Behind the Wheel
Convertibles

Simply put, convertibles convert. They can be transformed from snug, weather-tight closed cars into open cars by the simple action of lowering the side windows and well-padded, folding tops. Buyers sought to project a youthful, adventurous image and called their cars "chariots." Driving was easier for women with the Oldsmobile convertible, right, equipped with power steering.

The 1958 Chevrolet Impala convertible boasted precise ease of handling, crisp steering accuracy, air springs and a low-slung frame.

To drive a Chrysler Imperial convertible was to find out how much younger you can feel behind the wheel. It featured auto-pilot, the 1958 version of cruise control.

Cadillac convertibles were the self-professed leaders in style, design and engineering. Every window of the car used safety plate glass, and factory prices began at $5,400.

Some of Ford's convertible models had soft tops that disappeared inside the rear deck. Others had a steel top or rear window that rolled down at the touch of a button. Base price for a Thunderbird was about $3,900.

Pontiac capitalized on the space-age craze with its ad stating "new car for a bold new generation."

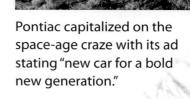

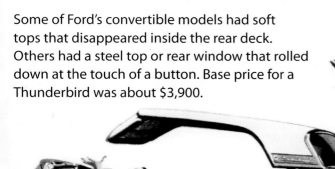

On the Job

1958 was a recession year. Unemployment remained high and rose to a peak in June when six of every 100 people were jobless, mainly because labor was being replaced with machinery. Wages continued to rise during the year, but rising prices wiped out all advantages of such increases. On the other hand, with advancements in technology, new jobs requiring specialized knowledge and training became available. Atomic power plants needed skilled workers. Technological advances in the automobile industry meant more jobs for qualified mechanics. Work was available in the field of research with the thousands of new consumer products being introduced.

Behind every new consumer product there were hundreds of research projects devoted to behind-the-scenes processes for industry. Probing the unknown, scientists were uncovering new knowledge in the areas of mechanics, chemistry and physics to make industry and products better than ever.

The American highway system continued to expand and provide jobs.

Men working in a 1958 atomic-age control room. If a nuclear reactor started to overheat, technicians had to have the knowledge to cool it off swiftly before disaster occurred.

Mechanics used up-to-date methods and tools. Expert training was important when it came to servicing cars equipped with the latest technology.

Electricity was being generated from atom-powered plants. Hundreds of electric company employees devoted their know-how to discovering the best ways to make atomic energy more economical in the future.

New telephone customers meant job security for the men installing telephone lines. About 1,000 more customers were added every working day due to the nation's booming expansion.

A top money-maker for major trucking fleets across the nation was the famous Mack truck, sold with a full range of engines—gasoline, diesel or turbo-diesel.

International trucks featured economy along with comfort and easy handling.

The Metro Daily News

FINAL EDITION

FEBRUARY 6, 1958

TED WILLIAMS SIGNS WITH BOSTON RED SOX FOR $135,000 A YEAR

This makes Williams the highest paid pro baseball player.

Watch the Chevrolet truck hustle when the farm harvest is hot and heavy.

On the Job

Rugged trucks

More trucks were needed for the continuing expansion of the Interstate Highway System. This system was a network of highways from coast to coast that bypassed towns and big cities to make traveling easier and faster. The Interstate Highway System also allowed goods to be shipped more quickly and that meant changes for truck manufacturers. Forty-foot trailers became legal and weight limits also increased along with the demand for more powerful engines to handle the loads. Rugged trucks could handle it all.

Tough, hardworking Chevrolet trucks meant business. They took "the teeth out of truck-killing jobs." As sure as it took more trucks to build the new highway system, the right truck for the job was a Chevy.

Oil was delivered by large trucks through all kinds of weather.

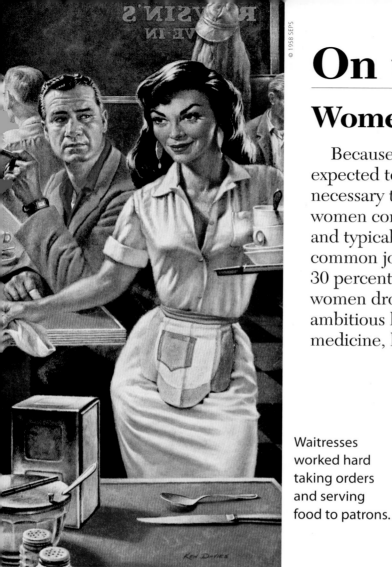

On the Job

Women in the workplace

Because of the well-defined roles of the time, most women were expected to serve as homemakers and mothers and it wasn't deemed necessary to pursue a college degree and start a career. Though some women continued to work outside the home, it was usually part-time and typically only after their children had entered school. The most common jobs by far were clerical, nursing and teaching. Only about 30 percent of college students were women, mostly because many women dropped out to get married. Women whose goals were more ambitious had a difficult path, though a few did pursue careers in medicine, law and the sciences.

Office work brought in money and sometimes included the connections to a future husband. This newly engaged secretary shows off her sparkling diamond to fellow workers.

Waitresses worked hard taking orders and serving food to patrons.

Clerical workers in 1958 used bookkeeping machines that increased speed and accuracy while reducing human error.

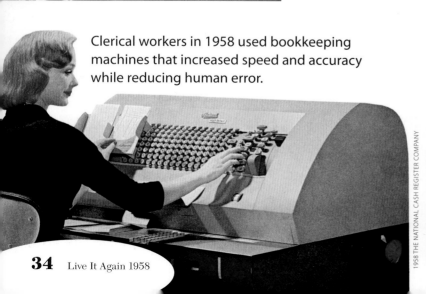

One airline required their stewardesses to be unmarried, age 20 to 26 years, no taller than 5 feet 8 inches and weigh no more than 135 pounds.

Teaching was an interesting and financially rewarding career. Most other job options were in the fields of domestic service, factory employment or clerical work.

FAMOUS BIRTHDAYS
Patricia Heaton, March 4 actress
(Debra of *Everybody Loves Raymond*)
Sharon Stone, March 10 actress

Airline attendants needed to be cool, posed and capable as they made arrangements for flights and tickets.

This secretary is pleased with the new Thermo-Fax office copy machine that produced dry copies, eliminating ink-stained fingers.

3.98

Cashiers were needed at most retail and grocery stores.

1958 Trivia

Q. What film did Elvis star in right before his induction in the Army?

A. King Creole

Rock 'n' roll singing star, Elvis Presley, was sworn into the Army in 1958. His manager, Tom Parker, made sure he served in a regular military unit rather than special services, so as to highlight his patriotism.

THE WEATHER
City and State—Rain, Snow, Colder

The Metro Daily News

FINAL EDITION

VOLUME 67 — NO. 101

20 PAGES   FIVE CENTS

MARCH 24, 1958

ELVIS PRESLEY INDUCTED IN THE U.S. ARMY

Elvis gained the status of U.S. Private #53310761.

United States News

On the national news scene for 1958, Elvis Presley joined the U.S. Army. Although fans complained that such a "national treasure" as Elvis should not be drafted, he was. The National Defense Education Act, passed in 1958, was a response to the Sputnik space satellite launched by the Soviet Union. Money was allocated for science education in high schools and low-interest loans for college students. Millions of American high school, college and graduate students benefited. The Nautilus, the world's first nuclear-powered submarine, departed Pearl Harbor, Hawaii, under top-secret orders to conduct "Operation Sunshine," the first crossing of the North Pole by a ship. On August 3, 1958, one of the Nautilus commanding officers announced to his crew, "For the world, our country and the Navy: the North Pole." With 116 men aboard, the Nautilus accomplished what had once been considered impossible—reaching the geographic north pole.

The nuclear-powered submarine, the Nautilus, is pictured on the night of its secrecy-shrouded departure for the North Pole.

It took four years to build the Mackinac Bridge to connect the two peninsulas of Michigan. The bridge was a magnificent feat of engineering and was dedicated in 1958. The dedication festivities included a parade of queens crossing the bridge in Oldsmobile cars.

Due to the race in space, schools across the nation received funds to improve science curriculum.

Using an artificial heart valve, like the one shown at right, surgeons could help thousands whose lives were restricted by "aortic insufficiency," or leakage in the body's most vital artery.

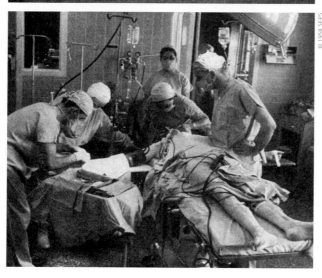

Advances in Medicine

Researchers quickly found that penicillin and other early antibiotics could not kill every illness-causing bacteria, and the term "superbug" was coined. In 1958, Vancomycin, a new antibiotic effective against staphylococcal and streptococcal infections, was fast-tracked by the FDA. Each year, doctors improved cancer treatment. Radiation therapy had been an important tool in the fight against cancer since the early part of the 20th century. In 1958, higher energy radiation beams for more effective cancer therapy evolved. More artificial heart valves, developed by Dr. Charles A. Hufnagel, were being used for heart patients.

High-level radiation improved cancer treatments.

The ultrasound was used for prenatal care in 1958, greatly decreasing the number of pregnancy complications.

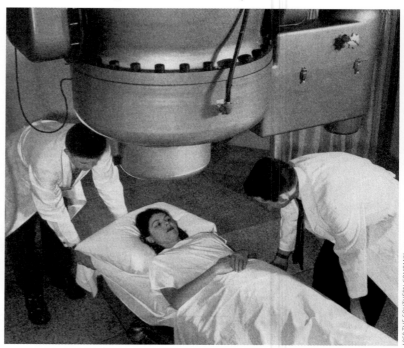

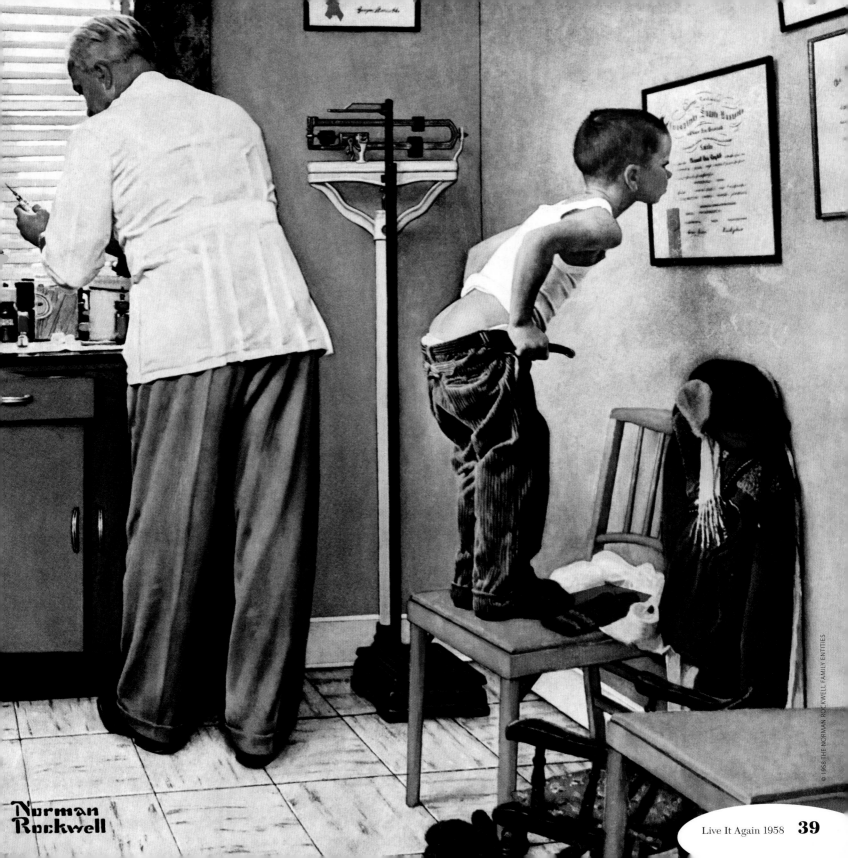

Norman Rockwell

Explorer 1 was launched in 1958, leading to progressively larger satellites carrying increasingly complex scientific instruments. The primary scientific instrument on Explorer 1 was a cosmic ray detector designed to measure the radiation environment in Earth's orbit.

The three men responsible for the success of America's first Earth satellite are shown left to right, Dr. William Pickering, Dr. James Van Allen and Dr. Wernher von Braun.

REPRINTED WITH PERMISSION OF UNITED STATES STEEL CORPORATION

NASA/COURTESY OF NASA IMAGES

1958 Trivia

Q. How much did the Explorer 1 satellite weigh?

A. Total weight was 30.80 lbs. Explorer 1 stayed in orbit until 1970.

The Race in Space

1958 marked a new era in the history of mankind—the Space Age. Familiar skies took on a new look when Sputnik, the world's first artificial satellite, was successfully launched by the Soviet Union in the last part of 1957. Americans reacted with shock and disbelief as Sputnik dealt a serious blow to the prestige of American science and technology. The United States hurried to catch up, launching the satellite Explorer 1 into orbit on January 31, 1958. Americans were relieved by the successful effort to match the earlier Soviet accomplishment. In July, the US Congress formally created the National Aeronautics and Space Administration (NASA). Headquartered in Washington, D.C., it consisted of about 8,000 employees with an annual budget of $100 million.

Activities in a blockhouse during the launch of Explorer 1.

An early space suit is shown being tested in North America's high-altitude pressure chamber in Los Angeles, Calif.

Studies and tests culminating in 1958 indicated the feasibility of manned space flight.

Diversity Efforts

School integration reached Little Rock, Ark., late in 1957, when a federal court ordered previously all-white Central High School to admit black students. This action resulted in a media event and considerable violence. In May of 1958, Ernest Green, one of the original Little Rock Nine students, became the first black student to graduate from Central High. Federal troops and city police were on hand, but the event went perfectly.

In 1958, while at a book signing in Harlem, Dr. Martin Luther King Jr. was stabbed in the chest by Izola Ware Curry. While in the hospital, King expressed no bitterness toward Curry. Upon his release, he said, "We should go out with determination to solve many of the social problems which contributed to conditions that lead up to incidents like this."

Civil rights leader, Dr. Marin Luther King Jr., converses with a man on a city street.

Members of the Little Rock Nine stand with their heads bowed during a church service prior to their graduation ceremony at Little Rock, Ark.

African-American protesters congregate at Brown's Basement Luncheonette in Oklahoma City during a sit-in while Caucasian police officers observe. The NAACP Youth Council began sit-ins at lunch counters to integrate segregated establishments.

President Eisenhower meets with various Civil Rights leaders at the White House in June to discuss desegregation. Pictured from left, Lester Granger, Dr. Martin Luther King Jr., E. Frederick Morrow, President Eisenhower, A. Philip Randolph, William P. Rogers, Rocco C. Siciliano, and Roy Wilkins.

Although electric pumps were being used on more farms, windmills still occasionally pumped water from wells.

In some areas of the country, people crossed rivers by ferry instead of using a bridge. A ferry was usually made of logs covered by a deck and was pulled across the river by a rope stretched from one side to the other.

Washing laundry for a large family required a full day's work, even with help from the children.

Country Living

Country living was a simple, though not necessarily easy, way of life. The family farm was an American staple in 1958 when a family could make a good living on less than 200 acres. Parents and their brood worked side by side and children learned a mutually beneficial work ethic by example. Farmers taught their sons to plow a straight furrow and tend to sick animals. Farm women demonstrated the correct way to plant a vegetable garden and hang clothes on the line for drying. There was a sense of satisfaction when viewing a pantry filled with home-canned goods or a barn crammed with sweet-smelling hay.

Apples are picked and squeezed into fresh cider with a hand-operated press.

For a farmer, few scents are as pleasant as that of newly plowed land in the spring.

FAMOUS BIRTHDAYS
Alec Baldwin, April 3 actor
Andie MacDowell, April 21 actress

City Life

A typical downtown in 1958 was a combination of buildings constructed around the turn of the century, some fine art-deco structures built in the 1920s, and a few modern towers. Together they blended brick, stone and steel into pleasing patterns that formed a lively retail and office district. Almost everyone who lived in the city went downtown regularly to work, shop, see a movie, hear music at a nightclub, or call upon a lawyer or dentist. Taxi cabs were the most popular way to navigate city streets, with over 10,000 on the streets of New York City alone. People also used buses, subways, trains and ferries to transport them to their destinations.

In spring, even in New York City, a man's thoughts turn to depleting the fish population. These well-dressed gentlemen are examining the latest in fishing gear in this Abercrombie & Fitch sporting-goods store.

New York City is filled with soaring skyscrapers and glass and steel towers that were built after World War II.

Apartments built one on top of another stretch toward the sky, but that doesn't stop this innovative boy from flying his kite.

Mom and dad are ready for a long-anticipated evening out on the town, but junior is not cooperating.

These Philadelphia commuters shiver as they wait for buses to take them to their own dry homes. When snow falls in the city, it is considered a nuisance for travelers and shopkeepers alike.

The Metro Daily News

THE WEATHER
City and State—Rain.
Snow, Colder

FINAL
EDITION

20 PAGES   FIVE CENTS

VOLUME 87 — No. 161

APRIL 3, 1958

SAY, DARLING OPENS AT ANTA THEATER, NEW YORK CITY

This performance is the first of 332 given at the ANTA Theater.

Moviegoers throng to the big screens of drive-in theaters to see actor Charlton Heston as Moses in *The Ten Commandments*. Families could pack up the kids and buy lots of popcorn for a cheap evening of entertainment.

Drag-racers surge at high speeds in short runs.

Dad, Mom and the kids gather around the organ to enjoy an evening of sing-along music.

REPRINTED WITH PERMISSION OF HAMMOND SUZUKI USA, INC.

Favorite Pastimes

Americans relaxed, comfortable in their new prosperity and the many conveniences that granted more leisure time. There were many ways to unwind after work. Bowling was the country's leading participation sport, with bright, modern establishments that featured fully automatic machines. Leagues of every description formed across the nation. At a time when conventional movie theaters were closing by the hundreds, drive-in theaters flourished. Most had room for several hundred cars, but there were a few drive-ins that could accommodate as many as 2,000 vehicles. A widespread interest in drag racing emerged. Spectators stood for long hours to watch curious-looking cars roar by at speeds well over a hundred miles an hour.

Fishermen cast for bluefish, bass and cod at this scenic location in California.

Bowling is a family sport that is enjoyed by those of any age and skill level.

Tops at the Box Office

South Pacific

Auntie Mame

Cat on a Hot Tin Roof

No Time for Sergeants

Gigi

The Seventh Voyage of Sinbad

The Vikings

Vertigo

The Young Lions

Some Came Running

The Sheriff of Fractured Jaw

Separate Tables

Going to the Movies

Hollywood stars kept the old magic alive at the movie theater, despite the increasing numbers of Americans who chose to stay home with their televisions. The movie *South Pacific* was tops at the box office in 1958. The film *Gigi* was awarded Best Picture at the Academy Awards along with nine other Oscars. In this turn-of-the-century Cinderella story a rich playboy, actor Louis Jordan, and youthful courtesan-in-training, played by Leslie Caron, enjoy a platonic friendship that blooms into love. The star power of actors Elizabeth Taylor and Paul Newman drew moviegoers to theaters to see *Cat on a Hot Tin Roof*, about an alcoholic ex-football player who drinks his days away and resists the affections of his wife, Maggie. The movie was nominated for six Oscars.

©GETTY I

This photo was taken during the "I'm Gonna Wash That Man Right Outa My Hair" scene of *South Pacific*. Mitzi Gaynor, right front, sang the famous song. On a South Pacific island during World War II, love bloomed between a young nurse, portrayed by Mitzi Gaynor, and a secretive Frenchman, actor Rossano Brazzi, who was being courted for a dangerous U.S. military mission. The movie won Oscars for Best Sound, Best Cinematography and Best Music. The music and lyrics were written by dynamic duo, Rodgers and Hammerstein.

THE FIRST LERNER-LOEWE MUSICAL SINCE "MY FAIR LADY"

GiGi

M-G-M Presents
AN ARTHUR FREED PRODUCTION

Starring
LESLIE CARON
MAURICE CHEVALIER · LOUIS JOURDAN
HERMIONE GINGOLD · EVA GABOR · JACQUES BERGERAC · ISABEL JEANS
Screen Play and Lyrics by **ALAN JAY LERNER** · Music by **FREDERICK LOEWE** · Based on the Novel by COLETTE
Costumes, Scenery & Production Design by CECIL BEATON · CinemaScope METROCOLOR · Directed by VINCENTE MINNELLI

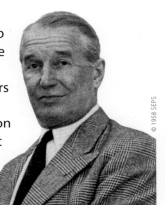

Maurice Chevalier, who played Honore Lachaille, was one of the stars of *Gigi*, the movie that won Best Picture at the Academy Awards.

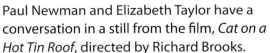

Paul Newman and Elizabeth Taylor have a conversation in a still from the film, *Cat on a Hot Tin Roof*, directed by Richard Brooks.

Actress Rosalind Russell, who played the part of Mame Dennis in the film *Auntie Mame*, was awarded a Golden Globe for Best Actress.

Actor David Niven won the Academy Award for Best Actor for his role as Major Angus Pollock in *Separate Tables*.

John Wayne, known as "the Duke", actress Eiko Ando and director John Huston on location for the movie *The Barbarian and the Geisha.*

Actor Robert Preston with his wife, Catherine, in their New York apartment. He was not known for his singing voice, but appeared in famous musicals.

Exotic leading man of American films, Yul Brynner, was best known for his role in *The King and I.*

"My empire is my face and my body," said actress Zsa Zsa Gabor. To many, she appeared as an icon of European glamour.

Stargazing Hollywood Style

Hollywood stars were often scrutinized by their fans. Perennial star, John Wayne, left his typical western set to star in the movie *The Barbarian and the Geisha*, filmed far from home in Japan. Wayne's salary for the 14 weeks of work was $666,666.67, a great deal more than the $75 a week he was paid for acting in 1929. Singer and actor Bing Crosby, age 53, found it difficult to guard his private life with his 24-year-old bride, Kathryn. Socialite and actress Zsa Zsa Gabor was frequently tabloid fodder, famous for her conspicuous wealth and lavish lifestyle.

Bob Hope and Carry Grant at a celebration after the Academy Awards. Both started out in show business as variety artists.

Seen at the Academy Awards ceremonies in 1958 were actor David Niven, rear, and left to right, Edith Goetz, Niven's wife, Hjordis Genberg, and actor Rock Hudson.

Newlyweds Bing Crosby and his second wife, Kathryn, perfect her golf swing. Playing golf was a favorite pastime for Bing.

Stargazing Hollywood Style
Famous families

Glen Ford, star of *The Sheepman*, shown with his son, Peter, said that what balanced his life was not play, but hard manual work.

Actor David Niven said, "I only pray that these boys will be as lucky and have as much fun as their father had."

Star of the TV show *Gunsmoke*, actor James Arness and his family lived in a modest home, with no swimming pool.

"I hardly get to see my husband, let alone dance with him," said Bob Hope's wife, Dolores. She got this chance at the 1958 post-Oscar party.

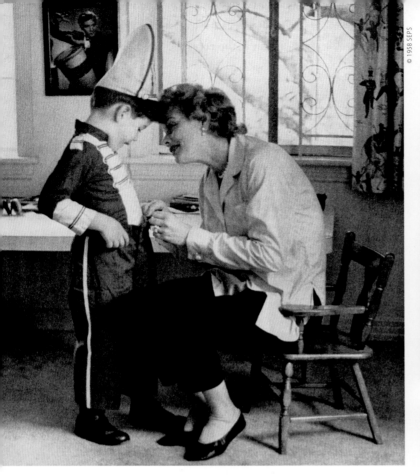

Television star Lucy Arnaz with son Desi Jr., who was born the same week as her TV show baby was born.

James Garner, star of the television show *Maverick*, said in 1958, "I'm still adjusting to the realization of quick success." He is pictured above with his wife Lois and daughter Kim, and below with baby daughter, Greta.

© 1958 SEPS

Singer and entertainer Vic Damone laughs with his wife and son. He is remembered for singing "On the Street Where You Live", from the Broadway show, *My Fair Lady*.

The Metro Daily News   FINAL EDITION

MAY 19, 1958

SOUTH PACIFIC SOUNDTRACK ALBUM GOES TO NO. 1 AND STAYS NO. 1 FOR 31 WEEKS

What Made Us Laugh

"But first—a word from our sponsor."

"It's a martini except I use chocolate syrup instead of vermouth, and milk instead of gin."

"The game was called because of broken glass."

"Since the Dodgers moved to Los Angeles,
he seems to have lost his will to live."

"Except that Monique makes her living in motion
pictures, I suppose we could be the young couple
next door on any American Main Street."

"How about changing sides for a while."

"That was a little better, now let's go back and try again."

Winners Spotlight

1958 had its share of winners and news headliners. Racehorse Tim Tam won both the Kentucky Derby and Preakness Stakes. Writer Robert Penn Warren was awarded the Pulitzer Prize for Poetry for his work, *Promises: Poems*. The best-selling fiction book of the year was *Doctor Zhivago*, by Boris Pasternak, and the top nonfiction book was *Kids Say the Darndest Things!* written by Art Linkletter. Jimmy Bryan came in first at the Indianapolis 500 and Marilyn Van Derbur reigned as Miss America throughout 1958.

American thoroughbred racehorse, Tim Tam, was considered to have a strong chance to capture the Triple Crown, but suffered a fracture while in the lead on the home stretch of the Belmont Stakes. This injury ended his racing career, but he went on to be a successful sire.

Pulitzer Prize winning novelist, Robert Penn Warren, works on revisions at his desk inside a paper cluttered barn.

Norman Rockwell painted Eddie Arcaro, millionaire jockey star of horse racing, for the cover of the June 28th, 1958 edition of *The Saturday Evening Post*.

A lead foot and an iron constitution are required to win the Indianapolis 500, as Jimmy Bryan discovered in 1958. His average speed was 133.791 mph and he narrowly avoided a terrible crash during the race.

Miss America, Colorado's Marilyn Van Derbur, is being congratulated by her family. After being crowned, Marilyn returned to the University of Colorado to graduate with Phi Beta Kappa honors.

Winners Spotlight
Basketball, tennis and golf

Masters Tournament Golf Champion Arnold Palmer is shown with his wife, Winnie, at the Augusta National Golf Club in Georgia. Palmer attracted legions of fans, known as "Arnie's Army", who hung on his every shot, celebrating his successes along with him.

NBA champions of 1958 were the St. Louis Hawks. The Hawks won the series in six games against the Boston Celtics. Standout Hawks player, Bob Pettit wearing No. 9, scored 50 points in the final game of the series.

©GETTY IM

The LPGA's biggest star and 1958 U.S. Women's Open champion was California girl, Mickey Wright. She said, "When I play my best golf, I feel as if I'm in a fog, standing back watching the earth in orbit with a golf club in my hands."

U.S. Open and Wimbledon winner was tennis great, Althea Gibson. She is noted not only for her exceptional abilities in tennis, but for breaking the color barrier as the first African American to compete in national and international tennis.

1958 Trivia

Q. What year was Althea Gibson elected to the International Tennis Hall of Fame? Was it 1964, 1968 or 1971?

A. 1971

Ashley Cooper, left, and Neale Fraser were the 1958 Wimbledon finalists. Cooper won in four games and also won the Australian Open and U.S. Open tennis championships.

Winners Spotlight

We are the champs

Champion Sugar Ray Robinson, right, fighting Carmen Basilio during the World Middleweight boxing match. Robinson was the first boxer in history to win a divisional world championship five times.

Baltimore Colts' star quarterback, Johnny Unitas wearing No. 19, throws one of his characteristic "last gasp" passes in this photo. This 1958 NFL Championship game between the Baltimore Colts and New York Giants, is known in football lore as "the greatest game ever played," with the Colts securing the NFL title. After a sudden death overtime, the final score was Colts 23, Giants 17.

The New York Yankees celebrate winning the 1958 World Series in seven games against the Milwaukee Braves. For the second time in Series history, a team came back to win after being down three games to one. Yogi Berra played in his 61st World Series game and collected his 61st hit, both World Series records.

Maurice 'Rocket' Richard, left, and Jean Beliveau, the stars of the Montreal Canadiens' 1958 Stanley Cup victory, hold the fabled trophy wearing big smiles. The Canadiens won 4-2 against the Boston Bruins for their third straight Cup victory.

The President welcomes the Nixons back from their South American "good will" tour.

Enjoying a little break from his duties, President Eisenhower is very proud of the fish that didn't get away.

Mr. President, Dwight D. Eisenhower

President Eisenhower struggled with difficult national and international problems in 1958. When rebellion in Iraq threatened to spread to Lebanon, the President quickly answered the Lebanese appeal for help. He sent thousands of troops into Lebanon. President Eisenhower and Vice President Nixon campaigned briskly for a Republican victory in the November congressional elections, but the party was hard-hit by an overwhelming defeat at the polls. The President called for patience with school integration while warning that all Americans must obey the rulings of the Supreme Court. He enjoyed good health throughout 1958, after recovering from a mild stroke in November, 1957.

President Eisenhower's family gather to celebrate his 68th birthday. They are, left to right; the President, wife Mamie, grandchildren Anne and David, daughter-in-law Barbara and son, John.

Ike's beloved pet Weimaraner, Heidi, and Thomas Stephens, his appointment secretary.

The President after an official greeting ceremony in the White House's Rose Garden.

The Brussels World's Fair was the World's first since World War II. The fair drew about 45,000,000 visitors and 47 nations had exhibitions. The Atomium, shown above, was the central theme of the fair, representing the enlarged atom of a metal crystal. It was described as the century's most daring architectural feat.

1958 Trivia

Q. What was the name of the Soviet dog featured in the photograph on this page?

A. Tziganka

The Soviets kept the pressure on the Americans in the space race, claiming to have successfully sent two dogs to an altitude of 280 miles and safely returned them to Earth.

World Events

In 1958, Nikita Khrushchev emerged as top man in the Kremlin and was named premier of the Soviet Union. Soviet writer Boris Pasternak was awarded the Nobel Prize for Literature for his efforts, especially his novel, *Dr. Zhivago*. Pressure from Khrushchev and the Soviet government forced Pasternak to decline the award because his masterpiece was considered out of line with Russia's Communist Party. It was also in 1958 that Egyptian President Gamal Abdel Nasser met with President Shukri el Kuwatly of Syria and merged into a single unit, called the United Arab Republic. For the first time, a passenger jet flew from London to New York, paving the way for world travel.

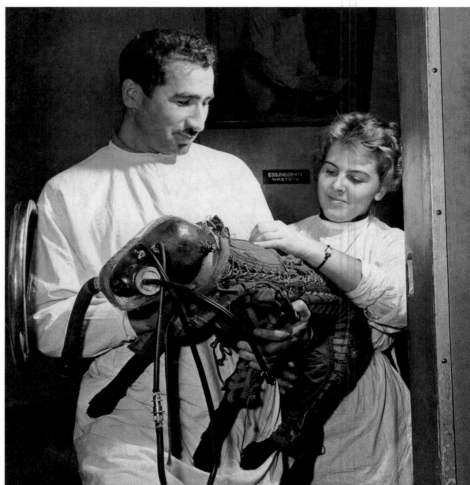

©GETTY IMAGES

Cardinal Angelo Roncalli, praised for helping save thousands of Jewish refugees, was crowned Pope under the name of John XXIII. He succeeded Pope Pius, who suffered a stroke and died in 1958.

The Metro Daily News

FINAL EDITION

THE WEATHER
City and Region—Rain.
Snow, Colder

VOLUME 41—No. 161

11 PAGES

FIVE CENTS

JUNE 9, 1958

"PURPLE PEOPLE EATER" SUNG BY SHEB WOOLEY IS NO. 1 ON THE MUSIC CHARTS

The Saturday Evening

POST

January 4, 1958 – 15¢

A VISIT WITH LEO DUROCHER
By HARRY T. PAXTON

GLENN FORD'S Own Story

The Private Life of a Great Artist: PABLO PICASSO
8 PAGES OF EXCLUSIVE PHOTOGRAPHS *By David Douglas Duncan*

The Saturday Evening

POST

March 29, 1958 – 15¢

RELIGION ON THE CAMPUS
THE MAIL-ORDER SWINDLERS ARE AFTER YOUR DOLLARS
Jack Sanford of the Phillies

The Saturday Evening

POST

May 17, 1958 – 15¢

THE GERM THAT HAUNTS HOSPITALS
A Visit With JACK DEMPSEY

ART and HUMAN DIGNITY
By Francis Henry Taylor

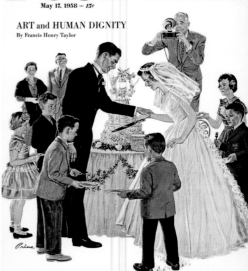

Post Covers by Benjamin Kimberly Prins

Benjamin Kimberly Prins was born in Leiden, Holland in 1902. Prins studied at the New York School of Fine and Applied Arts and Art Students League. Most of his career was spent in Wilton, Conn. He illustrated 34 covers for *The Saturday Evening Post* and also painted covers for *McCalls*, *Good Housekeeping*, *Readers Digest* and other magazines. His style was realism, representing the flavor of the time. A member of The Society of Illustrators and The Art Director's Club, Prins enjoyed a long career illustrating covers and features as well as advertisements for many major companies. He died in New Canaan, Conn. in 1980.

Falling in Love

For many young men and women, the idea of real love, to have and to hold, was a dream persistently pursued. The average age for marriage was 22 for men and 20 for women, so dating began at a young age. Couples would meet for coffee or a soda and hot dog. Boys and girls also made dates to grab themselves a burger and fries in a soda drugstore with a benevolent proprietor called something like "Doc" or "Pop." Then they would motor to a drive-in movie. To be alone, couples often went for walks in parks or on the beach. Then, for the lucky ones, came that real thing called love.

At long last, a sweet romance in the small universe of two in love.

The sport of bowling played a role in bringing many couples together.

A couple strolls through the local fair.

This couple escapes the crowded city to be alone on a rocky urban overlook.

Taking a convertible ride with your favorite girl was always a highlight.

FAMOUS BIRTHDAYS
Bill Watterson, July 5 comic strip cartoonist (*Calvin and Hobbes*)
Kevin Bacon, July 8 actor

"I guess she's ready to announce her engagement."

Bob Schroeter

Post-wedding joy is captured in this photograph.

Brides and grooms gather in June at this popular Pennsylvania rose garden.

Laughing, this couple removes from their car the decorations that declare them to be newly married.

Falling in Love

Becoming Mr. and Mrs.

The 1958 wedding dress was extremely modest. The dress tended to be ankle-length with sleeves and few embellishments. Lace was all the rage and dresses emphasized the waist. Popularized by celebrities, the hour glass figure was the style and crinolines were worn under dresses to accentuate it. The utmost in correct formal attire was expected for the groom and his ushers. The groom's attire was to match the formality of the bride's gown, as it was her dress that set the tone of the wedding.

Brides wanted lovely gowns and large wedding cakes. An average wedding cake in 1958 consisted of three or four tiers set directly on top of each other. This couple is ready for the ceremonial cutting of the cake while children crowd around eagerly awaiting their slices.

Our Homes

1958 was another year of unusual growth in the housing industry. The suburbs continued to expand. Many earned the title of homeowner, pleased to be able to nestle the family in comfortable new quarters at an affordable price. Yet looking out the front door, owners saw the house across the street, nearly identical to their own. Homeowners exerted their own personalities in other ways. If the neighbors planted an oak in their front yard, a maple was planted in yours. If they added green shutters, you added window boxes. In particular, the decor of the interior of the home established individual tastes.

Diaper service trucks line a suburban street, sharing it with the mothers and babies they service.

The children need another room, so Father's beloved den decor is converted from a fishing theme to juvenile bunnies.

The family room was devoted to the various interests and activities of the occupants, reflecting the increase in leisure time. Storage space was an important feature in the many small homes of the day. The kitchen remained the heartbeat of the home and was designed to save hundreds of steps every day. Some new bathroom fixtures were hung from the wall, saving space. Black and white floors, like the one in the kitchen above, were very fashionable and preferred by decorators.

New 1958 General Electric Dryer Gives You Perfect, All-Automatic Drying for All Washables!

Dries a typical load of family wash in less than 35 minutes

Model DA-920R General Electric Dryer illustrated about $2.80 per week.* General Electric Company, Louisville 1, Ky.

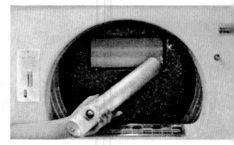

Automatic Sprinkler...dampens shirts, dresses, starched pieces ... has them ready for easy ironing in minutes.

BEFORE   AFTER

Automatic De-Wrinkler "tumble presses" properly tailored synthetic garments —even smooths out wrinkles caused by wearing

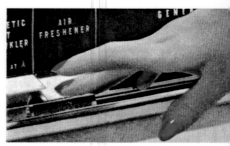

Air Freshener releases a gentle fragrance into air stream—gives clothes a fresh, breezy-day fragrance.

Automatically dries clothes so soft . . . so smooth . . . so wrinkle-free . . . you'll have much less to iron! Use on either 115 volts or 230 volts . . . the automatic control provides correct drying times and temperatures for every load. For high-speed drying . . . (times shown) . . . and automatic de-wrinkling of synthetic suits, use normal 230-volt installation.

Other features, Foot pedal opens full-width magnetic door. Lint Guard catches all lint. Smooth, porcelain basket protects finest fabrics. In beautiful General Electric Mix-or-Match colors and white.

Progress Is Our Most Important Product

GENERAL ⓖⓔ ELECTRIC

After small down payment. See your General Electric dealer for his prices and terms. Most models available in Canada.

Our Homes

Appliances to make life easier

The floodgates of consumption were flung wide open in 1958. The image of abundance also carried with it a sense of patriotism, as Americans defined themselves in part by their newfound gadgets. All-automatic washers and dryers streamlined laundry duty and were available in a rainbow of hues, including pink. Dishwashers allowed more women to be the gracious hostess and hub of the family circle. The revolving shelves and roll-out freezers of the new refrigerator-freezers put all foods at people's fingertips. Rotisseries, toaster ovens, portable mixers and electric skillets were sought-after smaller appliances.

General Electric sold a refrigerator-freezer that had no coils in back, which meant no dirt-collecting waste space.

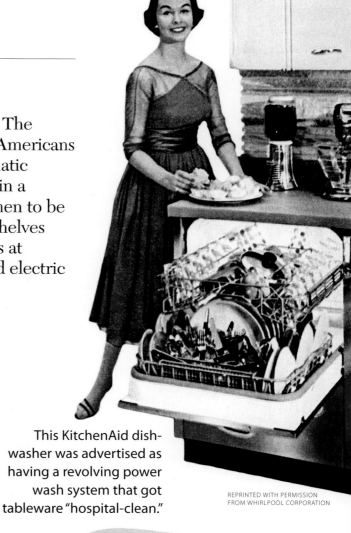

This KitchenAid dishwasher was advertised as having a revolving power wash system that got tableware "hospital-clean."

"George never lets me forget what a good provider he is."

Family Life

Instead of Mom, Dad and the usual two children, more couples opted for three or four children. By 1958, almost a third of all Americans were 15 years old or younger. Parents were eager to buy cars, houses, furniture and all the other material goods needed to set up a household in the growing middle class. Having children was considered the highest form of happiness. Women felt fulfilled and men were satisfied with their role as main provider for the family. Most evenings were "family night" when families shared, cared and had fun as a unit.

The entire family marvels at the sight of the new puppies the family dog birthed.

In a typical scene of a family yard, Dad and the boys use lawn mower parts to build a three-wheel suspension vehicle while Mom carries in newly purchased groceries to stock the kitchen.

FAMOUS BIRTHDAYS
"Beautiful" Bobby Eaton, August 14 wrestler
Scott Hamilton, August 28 figure skater (Olympic gold-1984)
Michael Jackson, August 29 King of Pop entertainment legend

Dad proudly shows off his new offspring to thrilled grandparents.

The children haven't been frightened by Papa's snoring, but by loud sounds of a thunderstorm. So mother will gather them in her arms and love away their fear.

Sweet and sticky roasted marshmallows and a round of tummy tickling fills a family evening at home.

Mom oversaw her children's musical development.

Teaching daughter the finer points of clean-up after a meal.

Mom cleverly allows little Johnny to wear his scuba gear during bath time to take his mind off the main purpose— getting clean.

Home-cooked meals were served to her hungry brood.

Many mothers sewed the family's clothing.

Family Life

Mom's busy schedule

First Lady Mamie Eisenhower said that women's lives "revolve around our men, and that is the way it should be." That phrase would be fighting words in today's society of independent women. The woman of 1958, however, relished her role. What other job had the variety of being a housewife? Bathing squirming children, sewing the family's clothes and creating a delicious meal served in style required a certain finesse. A woman's work was, indeed, never done. She read to her children to pave the way for literacy, encouraged development of hobbies and was Dr. Mom, available at all hours. What a wonder she was.

Mother and daughter relish the warm weather of summer in bare feet during a session of swinging.

Reading bedtime stories is a wonderful way to end the day.

Norman Rockwell

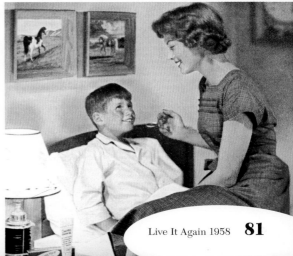

Mom is available, day or night, to treat discomforts.

Role Models

True role models are those who possess the qualities we would like to have and who have affected us in a way that makes us want to become better people. Members of the community were readily available role models in the way they cared for their families and friends and in the smiles and encouragement they offered. Models for healthy behavior were frequently parents or other family members as they guided us in making the right choices for our lives.

Norman Rockwell

Dad models the way to stay young at heart by riding the carousel with his son.

Through daily tasks performed lovingly, mother is daughter's example of how to care for a family.

Dad introduces his son to the new baby, paving the way for a future father.

Grandpa shares his wisdom during hobby time.

Children feel safe when led across the street by the friendly school crossing guard.

Dad demonstrates perfect kite-flying form for the boys.

The Metro Daily News

FINAL EDITION

AUGUST 29, 1958

FOURTEEN YEAR-OLD GEORGE HARRISON JOINS SINGING GROUP QUARRYMEN

John Lennon and Paul McCartney were also a part of this group. In 1960, this quartet became known as The Beatles.

Going to church was "the thing to do" among college students, but it became far more than a fad.

Families worshipped together in churches across the country.

Baptism is an outward sign of inner commitment.

Our Faith

The face of religion was changing in 1958 and revival fervor was apparent in many areas. During a three-day revival in San Francisco in 1958, the Rev. Billy Graham drew nearly 700,000 people. Church attendance was up and membership grew to 60 percent of the population. This was also a time of enormous activity in the construction of religious buildings featuring contemporary architecture. With few exceptions, all faiths and denominations came to feel that they needed to share their beliefs in words and deeds related to present-day life and conditions.

Parishioners pray for rain to renew farm crops and linger at the church doorway to watch the falling precipitation.

Revival in religious faith at colleges came as a surprise to the older generation who thought of universities as places where church ties were weakened.

Faith was also passed along through the written Word.

Shopping

Shoppers visited bakeries, grocery stores, hat shops, pharmacies and swank boutiques in 1958. But department and five-and-dime stores were the two places most typically and fondly remembered. The downtown department store was a community institution and a city's prime place to shop. The department store offered attentive service, first-class goods and an atmosphere of comfort. Saleswomen ran the floors and worked closely with shoppers. Elevator operators called out the departments on each floor. The concept of the variety store originated with items that could be bought for a nickel or a dime. The five-and-dimes appealed to nearly everyone because of their wide selection of merchandise. Window displays featured everything from dolls, scarves and plastic wallets to shiny metal pots.

The World Series is being played, and shoppers abandon other store departments to gather around the televisions and watch the action.

1958 Trivia

Q. What was the average price for pork chops per pound?

A. 92 cents

The butcher offers a wide variety of meat cuts to a shopper planning her meals.

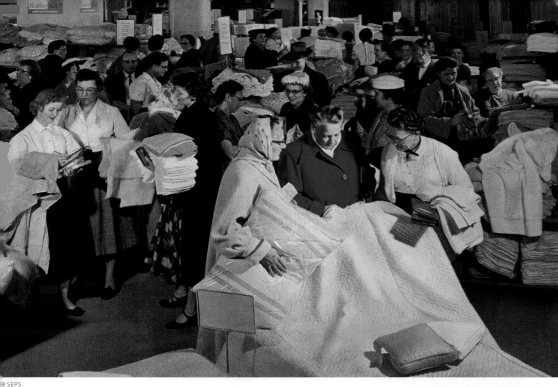

In January, "white sales" spring up across the country, with bargains to be found in bed sheets and pillow slips, towels and tablecloths. Women ignore aching feet to sort through the wares. Few men are courageous enough to brave a department store during a sale.

MEATS   PRODUCE

BILL HARRISON

"Isn't there a cereal that will sap their energy?"

Young boys pool all their money to purchase a doughnut to share. The smiling baker will likely give them more than their money's worth in mouth-watering pastries. Even the dog may be given a small sample.

Howard Johnson's roadside eateries offered a variety of foods to hungry families. Children could choose from meals such as the "Humpty Dumpty" or "Peter Piper" at half price.

Young boys sometimes have the urge to run away from home to see the world. Fortunately, this boy stops at a neighborhood restaurant and talks things over with a police officer at the counter.

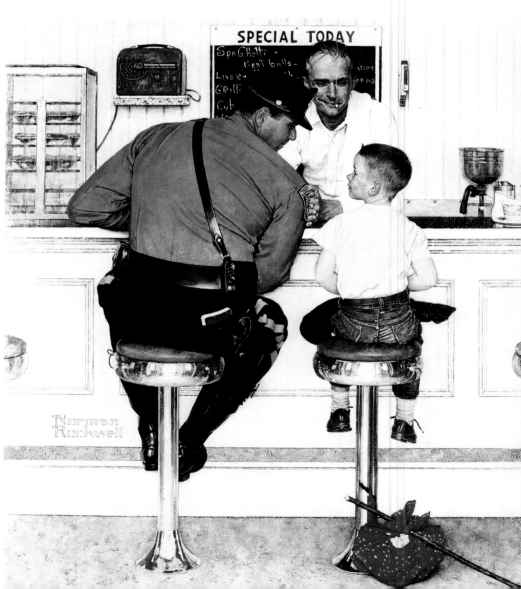

"What are you going to have for dessert?"

Let's Eat Out

Americans were on the move in their chrome-laden cars. When on the road, the public wanted restaurants that offered food in a hurry. In response, the restaurant industry promoted fast food that could be prepared and consumed, literally, in minutes. It marked a profound change in American living. A burger, fries and cola quickly became standard fare for millions of Americans. But not all fast food consisted of those popular three items. In 1958, Pizza Hut opened its first restaurant. Pizza had by this time become a rival to hamburgers as a favorite meal or snack. Diners continued to be favorite eating establishments for millions in this country, especially for breakfast and lunch.

A car hop in shorts and high heels takes an order from a customer at a drive-in restaurant.

This photo is of a nighttime view of a well-lit Stan's drive-in coffee shop in Hollywood, Calif., where customers are served food in their parked cars.

Traveling by Land, Sea and Air

In 1958 there was an explosion of transportation and travel options. The three states with the largest number of travelers were New York, California and Illinois. Airlines were carrying more people and plane travel was glamorous, on-time, hassle-free and exciting. There was also a 20 percent increase in overseas travelers, with more Americans heading for the Middle East and South America. Buses met the challenge of reasonably priced mass transportation for the growing population. The modern cruise era was born, with ships leisurely plying the Caribbean waters.

Buses could handle the vital, swelling flow of American passengers.

The modern cruise era was born in 1958, along with the first transatlantic air flight. Air travel was faster, but the ships weren't dry-docked. They found a new purpose plying the Caribbean waters. A whole new category of tourism was born—the cruise.

Airplanes included comfortable lounge areas where passengers could stretch out and enjoy conversation.

Although train travel was declining, railroads were advertised as a way to save travel dollars and avoid driving long, tiring miles.

American Airlines began to advertise an upcoming nonstop jet service between New York and Los Angeles, which would cut the travel time to four and a half hours.

Visits to family and friends who lived in scenic areas allowed even those with the smallest of vacation budgets to travel.

The station wagon has been packed for vacation and at last, the family is on the road. Thanks to the friendly Texaco attendant, this vehicle is ready for travel.

Swank motor lodges like this were Howard Johnson's latest project. The rooms were air-conditioned and many of the lodges had swimming poc

Family Vacation

Family vacations were the highlight of the year and most families went on vacation in the traditional months of June, July or August. Many families traveled by car, but some avoided long distances due to no air-conditioning and many congested two-lane roads. Yet an increasing number of adventurous Americans wanted to "see the USA in your Chevrolet," as an advertising jingle went. Common destinations were the Grand Canyon, Yosemite, Yellowstone and other national parks previously only read about or seen in travelogues. Accommodations varied from hotels and cottages to camping in tents.

In typical fashion, Dad applies brawn to the task of pitching a tent while Mom reads the directions. Will they be finished by bedtime?

This bird's-eye view of Disneyland was an awesome sight for visitors. Since its opening day in 1955, Disneyland became one of America's premier tourist attractions.

A boat pilot fires blanks at a mechanical hippo during this Disneyland tour. The setting was so lifelike; kids had a hard time telling what was real from what wasn't.

Scenic America

Americans were on the move and ready to see more of the scenic beauty of the United States. *The Saturday Evening Post* featured a number of picturesque vistas painted by artist John Clymer on the covers in 1958. The scenes drew flocks of travelers to the immense variety of natural wonders easily accessed through domestic travel. Many tourists chose to journey to national parks scattered across the country and tourism at parks and monuments more than doubled during this era.

For the May 10th cover, artist John Clymer painted the Yakima River in Washington State. "At this river bend father and son often fished for trout. … In case this lovely spot gives you ideas about temporarily leaving home, just off the bottom of the cover is U.S. Highway No. 10," writes *The Post*.

The Sept. 27th cover featured sage-brush-robed hills of the west. Notice the children in the foreground playing follow-the-leader. As was written in *The Post*, "These children, being sound of limb and imagination, are convinced that far below them is a wide, wide river. Of course, they've got to get to the other side."

The Metro Daily News

THE WEATHER

FINAL EDITION

FIVE CENTS

SEPTEMBER 5, 1958

DOCTOR ZHIVAGO BY BORIS PASTERNAK IS PUBLISHED IN THE UNITED STATES

The movie by the same title became a hit in 1965.

The Feb. 1st cover featured a painting of snow-covered mountains in the Cascade Range that extends from Washington and Oregon to Northern California. *The Saturday Evening Post* stated, "When the wind starts mellowing a little in the climbing sun, it will whisper to those southerly slopes that Jack Frost isn't really the man he used to be."

This scene of the Rocky Mountains graced the Dec. 13th cover of *The Saturday Evening Post*. "Jack Frost … and maybe a few other cool characters are tucking in the Montana Rockies for the hockey season," states *The Post*.

The artist was traveling in Washington State looking for a *Post* cover for the Oct. 25th edition, and came upon this stunning scene. Autumn's upcountry frost had painted the huckleberry shrubs with a scarlet-dipped brush and colored the maple trees orange and gold. His reaction, says *The Post*, was "Heavens to Betsy! Oh, my blessed aunt!" and similar expressions of adoration.

What Made Us Laugh

"I have a feeling he's going to make an excellent husband."

"Are you mine?"

"Now can I join the circus?"

"It's a wonderful location on those mornings
when you feel you can't get started."

"Don't be silly, Edna. What in heaven's
name would I be doing in anything casual?"

"As a matter of fact, I overslept myself!"

"If I were you I'd do something for that throat, dear."

"… And that was the supersonic whistle
you'll find in each and every box!"

Children who put their minds to it can have just as much fun at grown-up social functions as the old folks.

Thornton Utz

Boy and dog are happy with each other's company for this unique "sleepover."

Little girls practice their mothering skills with dolls and miniature strollers.

To Be a Kid Again

Oh, to be a child again, with a limitless imagination that transforms the ordinary into incredible adventures. A child's eyes see each day as fresh and new, filled with possibilities for exploration. Add a few siblings and some friends to the mix and ideas abound. Sure, we had homework and chores and had to endure a certain amount of bossing from adults, but for the most part, life was all about having fun. Childhood antics make for fond adult memories. Recapture the magic of childhood from your yesteryears. What jaunts bring a smile back to your face?

For Dad, it's just another ride on the carousel. For Junior, the horses gallop like the wind and he has become his favorite Western hero, complete with toy gun and cowboy hat.

Sometimes it's hard to contain all the excitement that a birthday party generates.

Even though the newly caught fish is small, to these boys it has all the makings of a meal fit for a king.

Play and Make Believe

Fictional western heroes galloped into America's homes and dominated both the TV screen and children's imaginations. Kids couldn't wait to buy the coonskin caps popularized on the *Davy Crockett* program. Countless boys even slept in their hats. Also sought after were the white hat, black mask, and revolvers of the Lone Ranger. On rainy days, many boys assembled plastic models. Aircrafts were the most popular models, but cars and ships were also top sellers. Boys were so proud of these creations that they were displayed and protected by plastic cases.

A boy tries on a coonskin cap that television frontiers-man Davy Crockett made famous.

Kids could pretend to be Superman, Zorro, Annie Oakley or Hopalong Cassidy with the right outfit.

Board games like Sorry were fun when the weather outside was uninviting, and sold for about $2 in 1958.

Boys enjoy operating an electric train set and are thrilled by the realistic choo-choo and whistle of authentic scale models. This deluxe model cost about $40.

Among space-conscious small fries, rocket, missile and satellite models were some of the most popular toys.

There was something wonderfully mysterious about wearing a Lone Ranger outfit and every boy was thrilled to dress like Tonto.

Pedal tractors were ideal toys for make-believe farmers and sold for about $30.

Play and Make Believe
Girls' Style

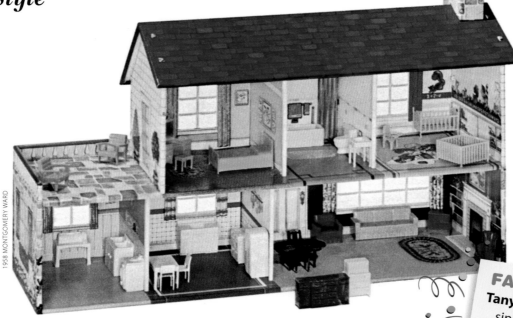

1958 MONTGOMERY WARD

This dollhouse had six spacious rooms and came completely furnished. It sold for $3.98 in the Montgomery Ward 1958 Christmas catalog.

1958 MONTGOMERY WARD

Conventional dress-up dolls, like the ones being admired below, were the undisputed favorites.

Tiny Tears was an appealing doll that looked and sounded like a real baby. She drank from her bottle, wet her diapers, cried and came with all accessories for about $9. There were several different sets available. The set shown here is the same set *Live It Again* Editor Barb Sprunger happily received one Christmas.

Children could make real ice cream with this miniature kitchen gadget called the Frosty Ice Cream Machine that sold for $5.

The Hula-Hoop™ was the most popular American toy ever made and was introduced by Wham-O in 1958. It cost $1.98 and was so trendy that stores kept running out. In the first six months, Americans purchased 20 million Hula-Hoops™.

Whether pretending to be a bride, ballerina, stewardess or cowgirl, it was fun to dress the part.

Remember feeding the giraffes and watching the monkeys romp during your childhood zoo visits?

It's summer and scents of outdoor grilling fill the air and spark the appetites of both the guests and neighborhood dogs.

Today, the man is proving his love by roasting on the beach by his wife's side. Hopefully, tomorrow she will reciprocate by relaxing in the shade under a cool tree.

Summer Fun

So many summer activities to choose from, and such a short time to pack them all in. Dad didn't mind cooking when he could grill in the great outdoors. He sometimes even donned a chef's hat and apron for the occasion. Beaches were classic summer hangouts, filled with nicely browned bathing beauties and the occasional well-covered sun-sensitive soul who also wanted to enjoy the sand and waves. July Fourth brought parades, a kaleidoscope of sights and the rhythmic sounds of marching bands as they passed by. A trip to the zoo was a chance to encounter exotic species of animals, birds and reptiles not seen among the local wildlife.

This July Fourth parade is paused for a tire change, right in front of the mayor, other bigwigs and three no-parking signs.

Stirring up the water with high-speed craft is not a good idea when those fishing prefer calm and quiet conditions.

The Metro Daily News

THE WEATHER
City and Suburbs
Secr. Colder
Cloudy & Rain tonight

VOLUME 97 — No. 161

FINAL EDITION

70 PAGES   FIVE CENTS

OCTOBER 7, 1958

POTTER STEWART IS APPOINTED TO THE UNITED STATES SUPREME COURT

Stewart served until he retired in 1981 at the age of 66. He was succeeded by Sandra Day O'Connor.

Leading Ladies of *The Post*

Take a peek at some of the art inside the covers of *The Saturday Evening Post*. The Leading Ladies of *The Post* are a collection of images from regularly-featured steamy romance stories. Illustrators were challenged to interpret these stories on canvas and we have included a sampling of the Leading Ladies of 1958. The sultry fashion-forward heroines of the tales are featured along with the original article captions.

She was rich and beautiful and thoroughly dishonest. "You don't know what you're asking," he said.

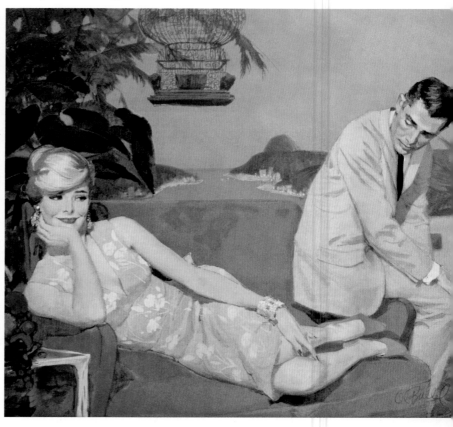

The only way she could get this great detective to take her strange case was to make him a witness to the crime.

"Just let me get clear of this lot," he said, "and I'll drive you back to London."

The whole gang was staring in shock at Connie.

"Barbaric," said Wayne gloomily, watching Candy charm four young men at once.

She was only a beginner, but for her the stakes were higher than mere money.

The red satin gown gave Evelyn the impact of a 20-millimeter shell.

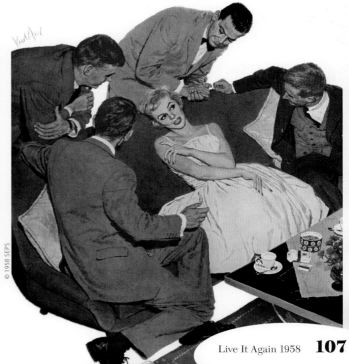

The season's smartest sweater styles were the chemise, a longer-line look, and the blouson. Prices ranged from $4 to $5.

1958 MONTGOMERY WARD

1958 MONTGOMERY WARD

This slim front chemise dress, with a semi-detached blouson for back interest, sold for about $13.

Brilliantly-hued plaid in 100 percent wool was in fashion in 1958. Dashing ankle-length pants were newly trimmed, slimmed and tapered, priced at about $15.

1958 Fashion

In 1958, most women chose to wear full skirts or perhaps a pencil-slim skirt and sweater. Pedal pushers or calf-length pants were popular leisure wear. The short box-jacket suit became a fashion classic with three-quarter-length sleeves. Women's fashion continued to endorse the idealized image of the happy housewife. The media used adjectives like soft, charming and feminine to describe clothing. Eyeglasses became smart fashion accessories that glowed with color and sparkle made possible through the use of plastic.

Hemlines with new excitement at the knee were introduced, such as this dress with its marvelous pouf of a skirt made of pure silk. It could be purchased for $19.98. Gloves completed the elegant look.

1958 MONTGOMERY WARD

Matching accessories were grouped according to color. This copper-colored group created an extravagant look. The pointed-toe pump cost $8.98; leather belt, $2.98; and silk chiffon hood, $4.98.

new Toni
first permanent with a new result
hidden body!

Toni home perms included new conditioning liquids that resulted in hidden body that made hair look alive, never limp.

1958 Trivia

Q. Toni home perms weren't the only perms available. What were some other home perms we remember?

A. Lilt, Bobbi, Rayve, Prom and Shadow Wave perms

1958 Fashion

Just for men

Men became fonder of wash-and-wear fabrics. Clothes could be laundered by hand or washing machine and dried by machine or drip-dried. Men were more daring in their approach to colorful sportswear. Sweaters were more fitted and slacks had high waists. Trim, tailored suits had narrow lapels, three buttons and very little padding. Ties continued to be narrow, averaging about two inches. They were often striped and made from hand-woven fabrics. Colors for business wear were generally dark and subdued. But sportswear and evening wear favored bright colors and patterned fabrics. What was new in shoes? The latest look was the bi-colored shoe, in tune with the new casual way of life.

Silk was added to the blend of Dacron and worsted for suits. The new highlights of silk gave an almost frosty look to the fabric.

The Metro Daily News

FINAL EDITION

THE WEATHER
City and State—Mild.
Snow. Colder
death is duty impaired

VOLUME 87 — NO. 195

16 PAGES   FIVE CENTS

NOVEMBER 23, 1958

HAVE GUN, WILL TRAVEL DEBUTS ON AMERICAN RADIO

This radio show had the distinction of being one of the few series that started on TV and then aired on radio.

Shoes were two-toned and made from soft, natural leathers with simple Continental lines.

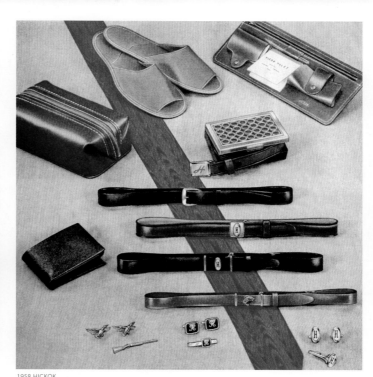

1958 HICKOK

Coordinating men's accessories were often purchased as Christmas gifts. Belts were priced from $3.50 to $5. Upper right is a visor valet for the car for $3.95. Tie bar and cuff link sets cost from $5 to $7.50.

Prices for men's coats ranged from $12.75 to $34.98 for this top-of-the-line imported Harris Tweed.

1958 MONTGOMERY WARD

Sweater shirts for men were washable, did not require ironing and were priced from $4 to $6.

1958 MONTGOMERY WARD

1958 AMERICAN CYANAMID CO.

Little girls' Easter outfits were only complete when a hat was added.

Boys wore the very latest in California-style sweaters for about $2.50.

Saucy French poodles and pom poms decorated this popular poodle skirt.

1958 MONTGOMERY WARD

Casual wear for girls paired matching slacks and pullover tops for playsuits that started at $3.98.

Washable and neat-looking, these jackets, slacks and sport shirts were made from easy-care Orlon fabric.

1958 Fashion

For the young set

By 1958, separate sections in catalogs were designated for teen girls and boys. This was the beginning of a marketing strategy aimed at the ever-growing baby boom generation. Girls usually wore dresses to school with matching knee or ankle socks. The popular "poodle" theme appeared on everything from skirts to scarves and wallets. Two-toned saddle shoes and different variations were popular for casual wear. Clothes for boys emphasized durability. Free jeans were sometimes offered if the knees wore out.

A group of teens, dressed in the casual fashion of the day, gather outside an ice cream shop.

Perfect for extra-special occasions, these "sister" dresses were priced from $4.98 to $5.98.

Plaid corduroy was advertised for preteens. The coordinating pieces cost $3.98 for the pants and skirt and $2.98 for the shorts.

School Days

Enrollment in schools skyrocketed as the baby boomers began their educational years. Many children attended kindergarten, but most went for half-days with the main emphasis on learning to get along with others. Average school hours for children were from 9:00 a.m. to 3:00 p.m. Many students got to school by riding their bikes or walking. The grading system for report cards of younger students was usually an "S" for satisfactory or "U" for unsatisfactory with check marks for achievement in the different areas. Older children were given the standard A, B, C, D or F. At recess, children's favorite games were four square, jump rope, hopscotch, kickball, tetherball, dodgeball and tag.

School's out for the summer, and children rejoice in their freedom from books and papers.

Teachers delight in school days like this one, when the students plan a surprise birthday party for their instructor.

"Kevin is sick and won't be able to come to school today. This is my father."

The day's events are shared in the hallway.

These youngsters pay close attention to the teacher's instruction.

There he goes, eager for his very first day of school. Mother and Father comfort each other at their son's milestone on the road to growing up.

Sometimes boys and girls paired up in elementary school, but usually girls were avoided because they had the "cooties," while boys were regarded as "disgusting" creatures. That mind-set quickly changed when the teen years arrived.

Tonight a girlhood dream, her first "formal" dance, will become a reality.

This teen girl earns extra spending money by babysitting instead of attending the New Year's Eve party.

A new hairdo and girl talk can work wonders.

The school hallway is the hub of social interaction for teenagers. At lunch and between classes, lasting friendships are forged.

The Metro Daily News

THE WEATHER
City and State—Boo,
Snow, Colder

FINAL EDITION

VOLUME 37 — No. 161

79 PAGES   FIVE CENTS

DECEMBER 2, 1958

THE 24TH HEISMAN TROPHY AWARD IS PRESENTED TO ARMY'S HALFBACK PETE DAWKINS

School Days

The teen scene

The word teenager was often used in 1958 due to the tremendous population of those in this age category. Middle-class teenagers lived in a small, comfortable world whose boundaries were the high school, movie theater, football field and drive-in. In some cases, the education that high schools were meant to provide was not a top priority. "I guess getting good grades is all right, if you do it on the side," a high-school girl told a *Look* magazine reporter in 1958.

Teenagers gained more independence and freedom and were able to buy more things, like food, clothes and music, with the increase in spending money.

Parents proudly watch their children graduate and take the first step toward adulthood.

Secrets were shared with friends via telephone.

"I thought you were safely tucked away in bed."

Christmas Memories

The Christmas season traditionally begins with a visit to Santa. Sometimes even the bravest of children become terror-stricken once seated on the jolly old elf's lap. Even the tiniest child knows that Saint Nick is a sweet old soul who drives a sleigh pulled by reindeer among the stars. But the first-hand sight of that huge beard can still be intimidating. At last, the anticipated day arrives and the family bursts into the room housing the tree and gaily decorated presents. Gifts are unwrapped with smiles and hugs bestowed on all and then it's time to sample the Christmas goodies.

© 195

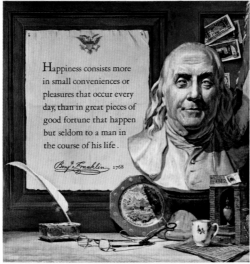

More *The Saturday Evening Post* Covers

The Saturday Evening Post covers were works of art, many illustrated by famous artists of the time, including Norman Rockwell. Most of the 1958 covers have been incorporated within the previous pages of this book; the few that were not are presented on the following pages for your enjoyment.

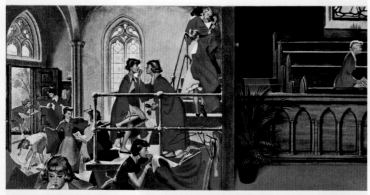

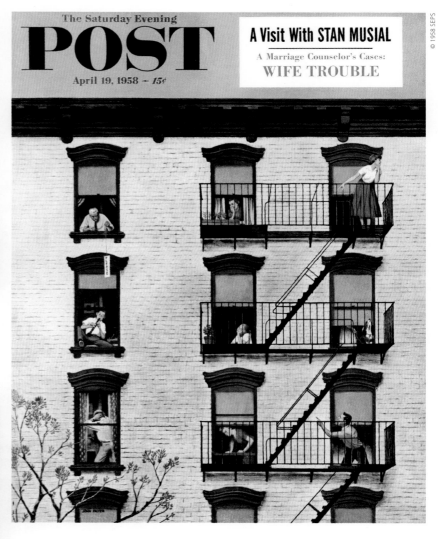

The Saturday Evening

POST

May 31, 1958 – 15¢

I CALL ON
LUCY and DESI
By Pete Martin

ADVENTURES OF THE MIND:
MAGIC EYES FOR MEDICINE
By V. K. Zworykin

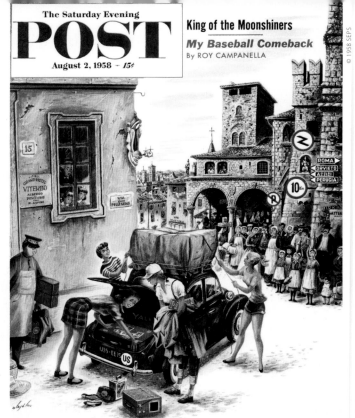

The Saturday Evening

POST

August 2, 1958 – 15¢

King of the Moonshiners
My Baseball Comeback
By ROY CAMPANELLA

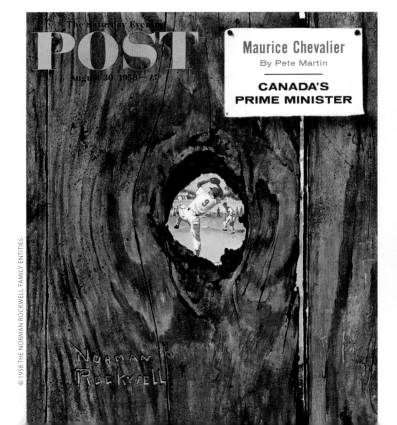

The Saturday Evening

POST

August 30, 1958 – 15¢

Maurice Chevalier
By Pete Martin

CANADA'S
PRIME MINISTER

The Saturday Evening

POST

October 11, 1958 – 15¢

BRET MAVERICK
By PETE MARTIN

Oklahoma's Bud Wilkinson
Defends College Football

The Saturday Evening **POST**

November 1, 1958 – 15¢

THE CALAMITY OF DIVORCE
A Case-History Report
By John Bartlow Martin

ADVENTURES OF THE MIND: **The Decline of Greatness** *By Arthur Schlesinger, Jr.*

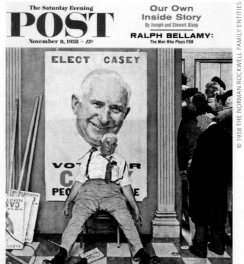

The Saturday Evening **POST**

November 8, 1958 – 15¢

Our Own Inside Story
By Joseph and Stewart Alsop

RALPH BELLAMY:
The Man Who Plays FDR

The Saturday Evening **POST**

December 20, 1958 – 15¢

How "Advance-Fee" Swindlers Victimize Property Owners
By JOHN KOBLER

January 4
Matt Frewer, actor (*Max Headroom, Doctor Doctor*)
Nina Foust, LPGA golfer
Andy Borowitz, writer

January 12
Curt Fraser, ice hockey coach

January 18
Jeffrey N Williams, astronaut
Larry Smith, NBA player

January 20
Brett Butler, comedienne (Grace of *Grace Under Fire*)

January 25
Dinah Manoff, actress (Elaine of *Soap*, Carol Weston of *Empty Nest*)

January 26
Ellen DeGeneres, comedienne (Ellen Morgan of *Ellen*)

January 27
James Grippando, novelist

January 31
Rafael Santana, shortstop (New York Mets, New York Yankees)
Tom Schuman, pianist

February 3
N. Gregory Mankiw, economist

February 6
Barry Miller, actor

February 10
Michael Weiss, musician

February 16
Lisa Loring, actress (Wednesday of *The Addams Family*)

February 17
Heidi Hagman, actress (Linda of *Archie Bunker's Place*)

February 21
Alan Trammell, infielder (Detroit Tigers)

March 2
Peter Arnold, architect

March 7
Alan Hale, astronomer

March 9
Jack Kenny, television writer and producer

March 14
Albert Alexandre Louis Pierre Grimaldi, Prince of Monaco

March 15
Laura Carrington, actress

March 20
Holly Hunter, actress
Rickey Jackson, NFL linebacker (New Orleans Saints, San Francisco 49ers)

March 21
Brad Hall, actor (*Saturday Night Live*)

March 25
James McDaniel, actor (Arthur Fancy of *NYPD Blue*)

April 7
Alexandra Neil, actress (Rose of *Guiding Light*)

April 9
Tony Sibson, boxer

April 14
John D'Aquino, actor

April 21
Kyle Stevens, LPGA golfer

April 27
Keith DeNunzio, rocker

April 29
Eve Plumb, actress (Jan of *The Brady Bunch*)
Michelle Pfeiffer, actress
Gary Cohen, baseball broadcaster

May 3
Kevin Kilner, actor

May 10
Ellen Ochoa, astronaut
Jeannette Kohlhaas, LPGA golfer
Margaret Ward, LPGA golfer

May 11
Walt Terrell, baseball player

May 12
Beth Maitland, actress (Traci of *Young & Restless*)
Eric Singer, drummer

May 18
Ray Donaldson, NFL center

May 20
Ron Reagan, radio host

May 21
Jefery Levy, television director

May 23
Mitch Albom, writer

June 4
Julie Gholson, actress (*Where the Lilies Bloom*)

June 6
Elaine Crosby, LPGA golfer

June 8
Stan Brock, NFL tackle (New Orleans Saints, San Diego Chargers)

June 12
Rebecca Holden, actress and singer

June 17
Bobby Farrelly, film director

June 20
Chuck Wagner, actor
Dickie Thon, baseball player
Ron Hornaday, racecar driver

June 29
Leslie Browne, ballerina (*Turning Point*)

July 3
Aaron Tippin, singer ("You've Got to Stand for Something")

July 10
Béla Fleck, musician

July 13
Joy Scott, jockey

July 14
Joe Keenan, screenwriter, television producer and novelist

July 15
Mac Thornberry, politician

July 27
Christopher Dean, Olympic skater

July 31
Mark Cuban, businessman and basketball team owner

August 4
Kym Karath, actress (Gretl in *Sound of Music*)

August 15
Rondell Sheridan, actor

August 22
Lane Huffman, professional wrestler
Vernon Reid, musician

August 24
Steve Guttenberg, actor (*Police Academy*)

September 6
Jeff Foxworthy, comedian
Michael Winslow, actor and comedian

September 10
Chris Columbus, film director (*Harry Potter*)

September 11
Roxann Dawson, actress
Scott Patterson, actor

September 16
Orel Hershiser, pitcher
Terry McBride, singer

September 27
Shaun Cassidy, musician and actor

September 30
Marty Stuart, country singer

October 17
Alan Jackson, country singer

October 20
Valerie Faris, film director
Lynn Flewelling, fantasy author

October 29
David Remnick, writer

November 1
Rachel Ticotin, actress

November 2
Willie McGee, outfielder (St. Louis Cardinals)

November 5
Don Falcone, musician and producer
Robert Patrick, actor

November 6
Trace Beaulieu, actor

November 7
Jack Wyngaard, dancer

November 10
Brooks Williams, musician
Stephen Herek, film director

November 16
Marg Helgenberger, actress

November 19
Terrence "T.C." Carson, actor

November 23
David Wallace, actor

December 2
George Saunders, writer

December 13
Lynn-Holly Johnson, actress (*Ice Castles*)
Clark Brandon, actor (Sean of *The Fitzpatricks*)

December 17
Mike Mills, bassist

December 19
Rick Pearson, PGA golfer

December 22
David Heavener, actor and musician

December 23
Victoria Williams, singer

December 28
Carlos Carson, NFL wide receiver
Mike McGuire, singer

December 30
Steven L. Smith, astronaut

Facts and Figures of 1958

President of the U.S.
Dwight D. Eisenhower
Vice President of the U.S.
Richard M. Nixon

Population of the U.S.
174,882,000

Births
4,203,812

High School Graduates
Males: 725,000
Females: 781,000

Average Salary for full-time employee: $4,817.00
Minimum Wage (per hour): $1.00
Unemployment rate: 6.8%
Rate of Inflation: 2.73%

DWIGHT D. EISENHOWER PRESIDENTIAL LIBRARY & MUSEUM

REPRINTED WITH PERMISSION OF EXXON MOBIL CORPORATION

Average cost for:

Bread (lb.) $0.19

Bacon (lb.) $0.79

Butter (lb.) $0.74

Eggs (doz.) $0.60

Milk (½ gal.) $0.50

Potatoes (10 lbs.) $0.62

Coffee (lb.) $0.90

Sugar (5 lb.) $0.56

Gasoline (gal.) $0.25

Movie Ticket $0.51

Postage Stamp $0.04

New home $12,750.00

Notable Inventions and Firsts

January 10: Chess phenom Bobby Fischer wins the United States championship at age 14, making him the youngest chess champion in history.

January 15: An annual Gallup poll of the most admired women in the United States gives top honors to former First Lady Eleanor Roosevelt.

February 9: Airman Donald G. Farrell begins a simulated seven-day trip to the moon in a flight simulator at Randolph Air Force Base in San Antonio, Texas.

March 10: A report reveals that Americans own some 47 million television sets, about two-thirds of the world's total.

April 13: Top honors at Moscow's Tchaikovsky International Competition go to American pianist Van Cliburn.

April 27: Evangelist Billy Graham kicks off his three-day revival at San Francisco's Cow Palace. The event will draw close to 700,000 people.

October 5: Joe Perry of the San Francisco 49ers breaks the career NFL rushing record of 5,960 yards set by Steve Van Buren.

November 10: New York jeweler Harry Winston donates the Hope Diamond to the Smithsonian Institution.

1958 Quiz Answers

1. Sparky, page 15
2. Tim Tam, page 58
3. Althea Gibson, page 61
4. Elvis Presley, page 36
5. Ford Edsel, page 25
6. Heidi, page 65
7. Johnny Unitas of the Colts, page 62
8. Everly Brothers, page 9

Sports Winners

NFL: Baltimore Colts defeat New York Giants
World Series: New York Yankees defeat Milwaukee Braves
Stanley Cup: Montreal Canadians defeat Boston Bruins
The Masters: Arnold Palmer wins
PGA Championship: Dow Finsterwald wins
NBA: St. Louis Hawks defeat Boston Celtics

©GETTY IMAGES

Live It Again 1958

Copyright © 2011, 2013 Annie's, Berne, Indiana 46711

PROJECT EDITOR	Barb Sprunger
CREATIVE DIRECTOR	Brad Snow
COPYWRITER	Becky Sarasin
COPY SUPERVISOR	Deborah Morgan
PRODUCTION ARTIST SUPERVISOR	Erin Augsburger
PRODUCTION ARTIST	Edith Teegarden
COPY EDITORS	Emily Carter
	Deborah Morgan
PHOTOGRAPHY SUPERVISOR	Tammy Christian
NOSTALGIA EDITOR	Ken Tate
EDITORIAL DIRECTOR	Jeanne Stauffer
PUBLISHING SERVICES DIRECTOR	Brenda Gallmeyer

Printed in China
First Printing: 2011
Library of Congress Control Number: 2011926658

Customer Service
LiveItAgain.com
(800) 829-5865

2 3 4 5 6 7 8 9